Little Wolf's Haunted Hall for Small Horrors

Tony Ross

Also by Ian Whybrow
and illustrated by Tony Ross

Little Wolf's Book of Badness
Little Wolf's Diary of Daring Deeds
Little Wolf's Postbag
Little Wolf, Forest Detective

For Heidi Philpott, a generous critic

First published in Great Britain by Collins in hardback in 1998
First published in Great Britain by Collins in paperback in 1999
Collins is an imprint of HarperCollins*Publishers* Ltd
77-85 Fulham Palace Road, Hammersmith, London W6 8JB

The HarperCollins website address is www.**fire**and**water**.com

1 3 5 7 9 8 6 4 2

Text copyright © Ian Whybrow 1998
Illustrations copyright © Tony Ross 1998

ISBN 0 00 675337 X

The author and illustrator assert the moral right to
be identified as author and illustrator of the work.

Printed and bound in Great Britain by
Omnia Books Limited, Glasgow

Little Wolf's Haunted Hall for Small Horrors

Ian Whybrow

Illustrated by Tony Ross

Collins

An imprint of HarperCollinsPublishers

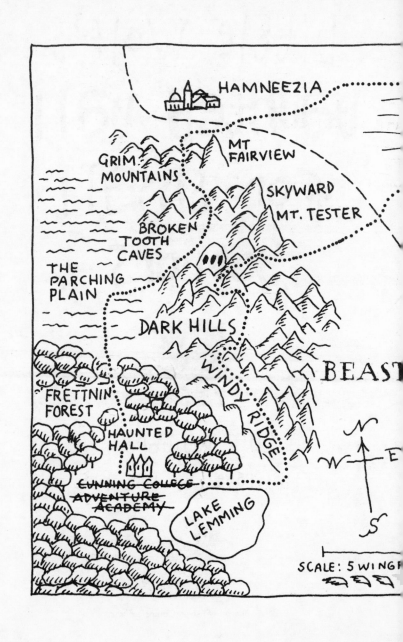

HAMNEEZIA

GRIM MOUNTAINS

MT FAIRVIEW

SKYWARD MT. TESTER

BROKEN TOOTH CAVES

THE PARCHING PLAIN

DARK HILLS

BEAST

WINDY RIDGE

FRETTNIN FOREST

HAUNTED HALL

~~CUNNING COLLEGE~~
~~ADVENTURE~~
~~ACADEMY~~

LAKE LEMMING

N
W   E
S

SCALE: 5 WINGP

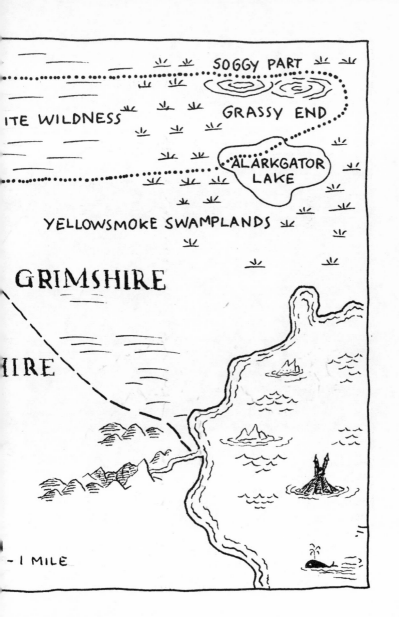

HAUNTED HALL
FOR SMALL HORRORS

THE BEST SCHOOL
FOR BRUTE BEASTS

HUNTING AND HAUNTING OUR SPECIALITY

Heads: LW Wolf and Yeller Wolf
Caretaker and Fixy Boy: Stubbs Crow
Small Horror: Smellybreff Wolf
School Spirit and Spook: Mister Bigbad Wolf. R.I.P.

Dayschool lessons: Hunting for Gold,
Spooksuit making, Flying ect.
Nightschool lessons: Walking through Walls,
Shocking for beginners and all that
Playtime: Hello Ween and Midnight Feasts

HAUNTED HALL
FOR SMALL HORRORS

Dear Mum and Dad,

Please please PLEEEEZ don't be so grrrish. It's not fair Dad keeps saying, "GET A MOVE ON LAZYBONES, OPEN YOUR SCHOOL QUICK." Just because he has fangache, I bet, boo shame. Today I will do news 1st, then cheery pics for him after.

Yeller and me and Stubbs are trying and trying. Paws crossed we open soonly. But did you forget our 1 big problem I told you about before? I will tell you wunce more. It is the ghost of Uncle Bigbad. He is fine, in a dead way, but he keeps being ~~orkwood~~ nasty, saying do this and do that or no more haunting from me. Just because he knows we *neeeed* him for our School Spirit.

Here is a pic of Haunted Hall, the scaryest school in the world (opening soonly):

I am not drawing a pic of Uncle Bigbad.
Because 1) he is too crool, and 2) you cannot
see ghosts, only after midnight (get it?)

I will draw me and Yeller, my best friend and
cuz, instead:

a is just us being normal (Yeller is the loud 1).
b is us dressed up as bossy Heads saying, "No
chewing in class," ect.

Now I will do Stubbs the crowchick:

a is him being all proud of 2 new feathers.
b is him doing looptheloops in his glowmask.

And now just 1 more:
a Small Horror of
Haunted Hall in his
spooksuit. Guess who?
Yes, Smellybreff, my
baby bruv, going sob sob
I want my mummy. (Only
joking, he likes it here really.)

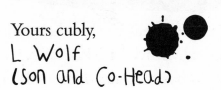

Yours cubly,
L Wolf
(son and Co-Head)

HAUNTED HALL
FOR SMALL HORRORS

Dear Mum and Dad,

Your crool letter says my pics are soppy and cubbish. I only did them to make Dad's fang feel better. Why o Y is he so cross? Because I would not do a pic of his horrible dead bruv I bet.

So all right, here he is haunting our cellar in the night-time:

He only comes if he smells lovely bakebeans cooking in the pot. HMMM, YES PLEASE, SCOFF SCOFF. He says they give him loads of Spirit Force.

Mum says does he still look like Dad? Well, he looks just like before he died of the jumping beanbangs. Only now you can see through him. He has a big horrible furry face, plus big horrible red eyes, plus big horrible yellow teeth and all dribble dribbling down. Also his eyebrows meet in the middle like Dad's, only more caterpillery. Plus he is all green, also ~~loomy~~ ~~looninous~~ he glows in the dark. He is v fearsum plus he makes your fur stand up.

He likes to come slidingly through the wall saying a terrible WOOOOO! and GGGGRRRRAAAH! Also he likes saying terrible words like this:

I AM THE GHOST OF UNCLE BIGBAD!
ME WOT DIED OF THE JUMPING BEANBANGS!
I DROOL, I DROOL FOR A LUVLY GOBFUL!
FETCH ME THE SHOVEL AND FEED ME SWIFTLY!

But if you say, "Uncle would you like to be our School Spirit and teach our pupils your ghosty powers?" he says:

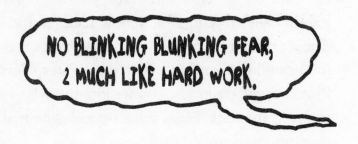

NO BLINKING BLUNKING FEAR,
2 MUCH LIKE HARD WORK.

Then he scoffs his bakebeans (canteen size) and off he vanishes.

Yours unhelpedly,
L Wolf (Head)

HAUNTED HALL
FOR SMALL HORRORS

Dear Mum and Dad,

Today Uncle said he *might* help us, but only if we hoover his grave. Also change the writing on his gravestone, boo shame, because it was good rhyming and true, saying:

Bigbad Wolf
is dead at last
he died of eating
beans too fast

Now he made us do:

Dear Bigbad Wolf,
We miss him so
Do not be dead
oh flip oh blow.
M. I. P.

Yours wornoutly,

15

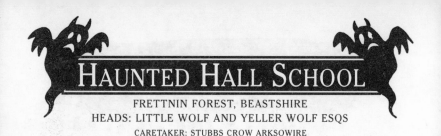

Haunted Hall School

FRETTNIN FOREST, BEASTSHIRE
HEADS: LITTLE WOLF AND YELLER WOLF ESQS
CARETAKER: STUBBS CROW ARKSQWIRE

Dear Mum and Dad,

Posh new paper, eh?

Uncle appeared again for a scoff of bakebeans. He said, **"TELL ME (SLURP) WHAT STYLE OF SCHOOL YOU WISH TO OPEN. IF I LIKE THE SOUND OF IT (GLUP) I MAY POSSIBLY APPEAR IN IT, YOU NEVER KNOW. IF I HAVE NOTHING MORE PROMISING IN MY DIARY (WOFF)."**

So we said our ideas for him:

1) Me and Yeller are the Co-Heads,
we can do all the Bossing About.

2) Stubbs is our teacher of how to make
spooksuits, plus flying lessons. Also he
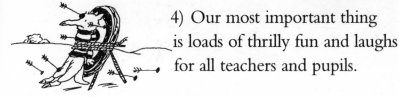
is Caretaker and Fixy Boy with
his clever beak. Plus he wants
to be Bell Bird by flying up to
the belltower and going ding
on the bell (saves rope).

3) Smells is just a Small Horror
(like normal, har har). Also his
ted can be if he wants.

4) Our most important thing
is loads of thrilly fun and laughs
for all teachers and pupils.

5) Loads of midnight
feasts of bakebeans
(Uncle's best snack).

Uncle said, **"WOFF SCOFF, AND WHAT DO YOU EXPECT ME TO DO FOR YOU?"**

I said, "Uncle, Frettnin Forest is a fearsum place for small brute beasts. Thus and therefore it is v handy to learn What to Do if a Big Scary Thing Tries to Get You. Also their mums and dads want them to be Splendid Tuff Horrors. So will you be our School Spirit and maybe teach us some tricks and ghosty powers? Like Popping Up Quick and Hollow Larfing?

Uncle said, "SNIFF SNUFF SNY,
WHAT DO I SPY? I SPY FLIPPING
FLOPPING HARD LABOUR! YOU WISH ME
TO SHARE MY SPIRIT POWERS? AND BE
A TAME TERROR TO TRAIN YOUR PUPILS?
GRRRR, NO FEAR! I HATE SHARING.
ALSO, I AM SO MIGHTY, YOUR SISSY
PUPILS WOULD NEVER STAND UP TO THE
SHOCK OF ME!!"

Yeller said quick, "UNCLE, REALLY WE WANT YOU SHOWIN OFF YOUR POWERS, NOT SHARIN. ALSO, CAN'T YOU TURN YOUR TERROR DOWN A BIT?"

Uncle said, "HMMM, (GLUP) SHOWING OFF? YES, I DO LIKE THE SOUND OF THAT, I LOVE SHOWING OFF. YERSS. WELL P'RAPS AND MAYBE I WILL CONSIDER. BUT YOU MUST DOUBLE MY RATION OF (BURP) LOVELY BAKEBEANS, SO GOOD FOR MY SPIRIT FORCE. AND YOU CAN TIDY THIS BLINKING BLUNKING PLACE UP, IT'S A DISGRRRRRACE!"

Not fair,

Yours discustardly,
Little

ps You say what is M.I.P. on
Uncle's new gravestone?
Answer, Moan in Peace.

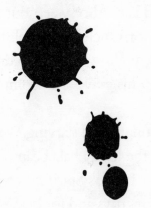

Dear Mum and Dad,

Phew, work work work! Clean the blackboard, flit the flies, polish the desks, shoo the spiders, scrub the floors, windows and lavs. Also sweep out the cellar so it is posh enuf for Uncle's grate self to appear in. He is a big lazy ghost, also a greedyguts 2. He only does lying in his grave and scoffing.

Us worky boys are hungry and starving. We're not even allowed to eat the lovely bakebeans because they are only for Uncle's Spirit Force. We were saving them for rainy days and for being poor, like now, with no money from pupils, boo shame.

So please send rabbit rolls and mice pies.

Yours rumbletumly,
Littly

Dear Mum and Dad,

The rabbit rolls and mice pies were
hmmmshus and yumshus. Yeller and me love
them, kiss kiss. Smells saves all the tails and
whiskers till last, then he eats them 2 quick and
gets a coff – so cubbish! Also Stubbs
says, "Ark," meaning thanks for
the cheese, it was ark-stra spesh.

But whyo Y do you say I have let the pack
down being poor again? Because who put
rockets under my safe and blew it up into small
smithers? Who made my gold go raining all over
Frettnin Forest so nobody can find it now?
Answer, your darling baby pet, Smellybreff. But
you never blame him, do you?

But now listen to *this* news, it is good. Yeller
has just made up a fine advert saying:

23

ARRROOOO! Look out Richness, we are after you again!

Yours chestoutly,

L Wolf esqwire

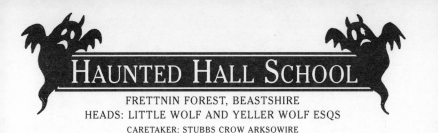

Dear Mum and Dad,

Will you write and tell Smellybreff not to be a ~~noosink~~ ~~newsance~~ pain. Because me, Yeller and Stubbs are trying and trying to please Uncle to get him to be our School Spirit and Terror, and Smells keeps messing all our things up. Also we must rush about pantingly, pasting up adverts all over Frettnin Forest.

Tell him he must just muck around with his ted like a normal small bruv. Not keep asking to be a Co-Head like me and Yeller. Just because he got his Silver Daring Deed Award for Clues and

Courage when he was cubnapped by Mister Twister. But he is still 2 whiny and hopeless to play teachers proply. What do you think?

Your busywizzy boy,

L

PS How about a nice surprise for us, hint hint? Like some Ratflakes or Moosepops maybe?

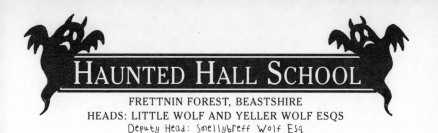

HAUNTED HALL SCHOOL

FRETTNIN FOREST, BEASTSHIRE
HEADS: LITTLE WOLF AND YELLER WOLF ESQS
Deputy Head: Smellybreff Wolf Esq
CARETAKER: STUBBS CROW ARKSQWIRE

Dear Mum and Dad,

Thank you for your LOUD REPLY in red ink. Ooo-er. So yes, you're right, Smells must have his own way. Plus he can have a Deputy Head Badge if you want, plus be a Sir. Yes, I do remember he is your darling baby pet. And tell Dad yes, I do know what GOING RAVING MAD means, so no need him coming on a long journey to show me. Thank you wunce morely.

Yours toldoffly,

27

HAUNTED HALL SCHOOL

FRETTNIN FOREST, BEASTSHIRE
HEADS: LITTLE WOLF AND YELLER WOLF ESQS
DEPUTY HEAD: SMELLYBREFF WOLF ESQ
CARETAKER: STUBBS CROW ARKSQWIRE

Dear Mum and Dad,

    I said Smells could be our Deputy Head like you made me. But can you just tell him "No more caning people" and "Stop saying bend over swish all the time"?

    Yours stungly,
       L Wolf (Head)

HAUNTED HALL SCHOOL

FRETTNIN FOREST, BEASTSHIRE
HEADS: LITTLE WOLF AND YELLER WOLF ESQS
DEPUTY HEAD: SMELLYBREFF WOLF ESQ
CARETAKER: STUBBS CROW ARKSQWIRE

Dear Mum and Dad,

Your photo of Dad saying PACK IN THAT CANING, PET arrived today. I showed it to Smells and guess what? It made him howl headoffly. Then he jumped in the cupboard and slam went the door.

I said to Yeller and Stubbs, "That was a good scare for him, he will stop hitting us now I bet."

Sad to say, he was just looking for some scissors. Now he has cut up your photo plus our curtains, tablecloff, ect.

Yours curtainlessly,
Little

29

HAUNTED HALL SCHOOL

FRETTNIN FOREST, BEASTSHIRE
HEADS: LITTLE WOLF AND YELLER WOLF ESQS
DEPUTY HEAD: SMELLYBREFF WOLF ESQ
CARETAKER: STUBBS CROW ARKSQWIRE

Dear Mum and Dad,

Good thing Smells found those scissors! He
says Cutting Things Up is his best thing now.
Plus Stubbs has trained him to do gluework. So
now Smells says we must call him Mister Sticker
and let him be a busy cub doing stickers all day.
He likes footballers best, so lucky there are about
1 millium *Wolf Weekly Sports* in the shed for him
to cut up and glue, eh?

Phew, now Yeller and me can do some proper
thinking up ideas for our new scary school
without *swish, ouch,* every time we bend over.

Yours cumfybottly,

L W

30

HAUNTED HALL SCHOOL

FRETTNIN FOREST, BEASTSHIRE
HEADS: LITTLE WOLF AND YELLER WOLF ESQS
DEPUTY HEAD: SMELLYBREFF WOLF ESQ
CARETAKER: STUBBS CROW ARKSQWIRE

Dear Mum and Dad,

Flip and blow. Putting up those adverts in Frettnin Forest was 2 days ago and still not 1 pupil has come. Y? I will say. It is because somebody has stuck Wanted posters all over them, that is Y! They are posters for Mister Twister the fox, saying:

WANTED
MISTER TWISTER
HE IS CUNNING,
HE IS NASTY
ALSO HE IS THE BEST
MASTER OF DISGUISE
IN BEASTSHIRE
—
BIG REWARD FOR CAPTURE

31

3 boos for a wopping, plopping fib! Because what about Uncle Bigbad? He is a lot more cunninger, crooler and worster. Also he is a brilliant dizgizzer if he tries his hardest. Plus he has loads of secret powers, I bet, only he hates sharing. Also he is 2 busy at the moment being a lazy loafer.

Yours insultedly,
Little

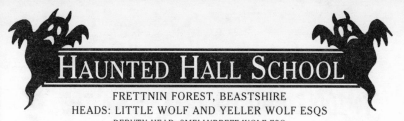

HAUNTED HALL SCHOOL

FRETTNIN FOREST, BEASTSHIRE
HEADS: LITTLE WOLF AND YELLER WOLF ESQS
DEPUTY HEAD: SMELLYBREFF WOLF ESQ
CARETAKER: STUBBS CROW ARKSQWIRE

Dear Mum and Dad,

Felt sad all day because Mister Twister's Wanted posters made our adverts feel Unwanted. But then Yeller had a brilliant idea! Make Uncle a bit jealous! Because then maybe he will want to show off and be more helping to us!

So at the bong of midnight, when Uncle came sniffsnuffingly after his best snack (bakebeans, canteen size), Yeller said justwonderingly, "I WAS JUSTWONDERIN, UNCLE, DO YOU THINK MISTER TWISTER MIGHT GET A LOT FAYMUSSER THAN YOU, WHAT WITH YOU LYIN IN YOUR GRAVE MOST OF THE TIME?"

33

Uncle said, "GRRRRR, THAT IS UTTER TWIDDLE AND TWODDLE, I AM THE GREAT STAR, FORMERLY KNOWN AS BIGBAD WOLF!! EVERYBODY KNOWS AND FEARS ME, I CAN DO FAR MORE CUNNING TRICKS THAN THAT MERE FOX! I CAN DO BUMPS IN THE NIGHT, I CAN DO WALKING THROUGH LUMPY OBJECTS, I CAN SMASH CHINA BY REMOTE CONTROL, I CAN DO GHASTLY HOWLS AND HOLLOW LARFS, NOT TO MENTION GOING HEADLESS AND OTHER MIGHTY SPIRIT POWERS LIKE FINDING LOST TREASURE."

Yeller said, "DID YOU SAY, 'FINDIN LOST TREASURE'?"

Uncle said, "GRRRRR AND BLARST! DID I SAY MY POWER OF FINDING LOST TREASURE? YOU MADE THAT SLIP OUT BY MAKING ME JEALOUS, YOU BLINKING BLUNKERS! WELL, YOU CAN FORGET ABOUT ME SHARING THAT POWER! JUST GET BUSY! FETCH ME CROWDS OF ADMIRERS SWIFTLY, SWIFTLY. I DESERVE THEM. SO THAT I CAN THRILL AND AMAZE THEM WITH MY MIGHTYNESS!"

Arrrooo! He is helpful to us at last! Must rush, new adverts needed!

Yours thinkythinkly,
Little

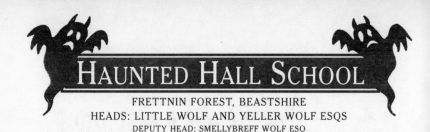

HAUNTED HALL SCHOOL

FRETTNIN FOREST, BEASTSHIRE
HEADS: LITTLE WOLF AND YELLER WOLF ESQS
DEPUTY HEAD: SMELLYBREFF WOLF ESQ
CARETAKER: STUBBS CROW ARKSQWIRE

Dear Mum and Dad,

Yeller and me did loads of new adverts. Phew, what a lot of drawing, also writing, colouring-in ect! All that work and no nice dinner after, boo shame (hint hint).

Stubbs did bring some chestnuts he collected from Frettnin Forest.

Yeller said all down and dumply, "THANKS, STUBBS, BUT WOLF CUBS DO NOT EAT PRICKLY CHESTNUCKS."

Stubbs said, "Ark Prrark," meaning they are not for eating, they are for prarktiss! He wanted us to go to the classroom and sit the chestnuts down at the desks. He said we could pretend they were hedgehogs adding up sums, then boss them about. Chestnuts do not put up their hands and call you sir, but true they are

36

v good for saying Headly things to, like "Tuck your shirt in, sonny."

Smells got jealous and says he is not Mister Sticker any more, he is Mister Woodcutter. So Stubbs made him a playcabin in the dining room. Also, Yeller let him borrow the chopper. Thus and therefore not much chairs and tables left, I fear. Maybe you want Smells back at The Lair quite soonly?

Yours beggingly,
Littly Wittly (snuggle snuggle)

PS This is a pic of what our larder is like (bare, get it?) Please send more grub: rabbit rolls, shredded shrews, moosepops, anything. Also something for Stubbs, and do you think you can find some tins of bakebeans (canteen size), we are getting short of them also, boo shame. Try looking for some in a cub scout camping place. But no eating them (the cub scouts, I mean) har har.

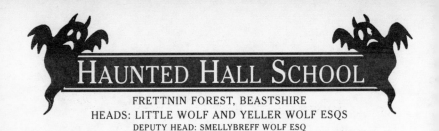

HAUNTED HALL SCHOOL

FRETTNIN FOREST, BEASTSHIRE
HEADS: LITTLE WOLF AND YELLER WOLF ESQS
DEPUTY HEAD: SMELLYBREFF WOLF ESQ
CARETAKER: STUBBS CROW ARKSQWIRE

Dear Mum and Dad,

Thanks for the grub. The Deerdrops,
Moosepops and Ratflakes were lovely, also the
Hamster Hoops and Goosabix. We like the
packets 2, yum tasty! Stubbs says, "Ark," for the
arkscellent Maggot Mix. No bakebeans? Pity.
(Don't tell Uncle only a few left.)

We have put up our new adverts in Frettnin Forest. Paws crossed there are no more Wanted Mister Twister posters to cover them up, eh?

I am writing my quietest and most notdisturbly because Yeller is making up something clever. A Kwestion Hare I think it is called. It is not an advert, it is a new way to tempt the mums and dads of Frettnin Forest to send small brute beasts to Haunted Hall. Also it is going to mention about our Entrance Test (our test to get in, get it?)

Arrroooo, Yeller's ideas are just the best! Because the mums and dads will say to their small brutes, "Oh goodie, a test for you, and you are such a brilliant cheater."

Yours mercybucketly,
moi (french)

HAUNTED HALL SCHOOL

FRETTNIN FOREST, BEASTSHIRE
HEADS: LITTLE WOLF AND YELLER WOLF ESQS
DEPUTY HEAD: SMELLYBREFF WOLF ESQ
CARETAKER: STUBBS CROW ARKSQWIRE

Dear Mum and Dad,

At sunjump today, Stubbs went highflying to
drop Yeller's Kwestion Hares all over the forest.
Paws crossed for many a reply. By the way, Yeller
says maybe some parents can pay in bakebeans
instead of fees, good, eh? Because that will help
keep Uncle a happy haunter.

I'm sending 1 Kwestion Hare for you to see.
A bit smudjy, sorry, Smells did a spit on it
(jealous), also Yeller's writing is a bit hilly.

Yours rushly,

Little

40

KWESTION HARE
ABOUT HAUNTED HALL
* ? * ? * ? * ? * ? *

IMPORTANT KWESTIONS FOR PROUD
PARENTS FROM L AND Y WOLF, CO-HEADS,
HAUNTED HALL SCHOOL, FRETTNIN FOREST
(DO YOUR TOOTHMARK OR TICK IN 1 BOX
ONLY)

CAN YOU READ? (TRICK QUESTION)
YES ☐   NO ☐   MY BRANE IS 2 SMAL ☐

HAVE YOU GOT MONEY FOR FEES (NOT FOR
FLEAS)
YES LOADS ☐
NO WE ARE A BIT SAD & POOR ☐

IF NO MONEY, WILL YOU PAY IN
BAKEBEANS?
NO ☐   YES, BIG TINFULLS ☐

IS YOUR CUB, PUP, FLEDGIE ECT JUST A
WEAKY?
YES ☐   NO ☐

DO YOU WANT HIM LEARNIN TUFFNESS OR
JUST CURLIN UP OR HIDIN DOWN HOLES?
TUFF ☐   CURL UP ☐   HOLE HIDER ☐

DO YOU WANT HIM LEARNIN GOOD
HAUNTY POWERS and SURVIVAL TRICKS
OFF OF A PROPER GHOST SUCH AS BIGBAD
WOLF OR JUST NORMAL BORIN LESSONS?
HAUNTIN AND TRICKS ☐   BORIN STUFF ☐

DO YOU WANT HIM BEIN A HORROR OF
hAUNTED HALL or JUST going TO A
RUBBISH SCHOOL?
hAUNTED HALL, THE BEST SCARYEST
SCHOOL IN THE WORLD ☐ ANY OLD DUMP ☐

WILL Your SMALL BRUTE COME for OUR
ENTRANCE TEST?
PROBLY ☐   DEFFNLY ☐   MAYBE ☐

IN A SHORT WAY, SAY WHAT HE/SHE/IT
NEEDS TEACHIN MOST (ANSWER IN BEST
PICS OR WRITIN, NO PAWPRINTS)

HAUNTED HALL SCHOOL

FRETTNIN FOREST, BEASTSHIRE
HEADS: LITTLE WOLF AND YELLER WOLF ESQS
DEPUTY HEAD: SMELLYBREFF WOLF ESQ
CARETAKER: STUBBS CROW ARKSQWIRE

Dear Mum and Dad,

ARRROOOO!!

Stubbs just flew in the window with a
Kwestion Hare filled in by a dad weasel! He has
ticked the YES LOADS OF MONEY box
(arrroooo x 3!) Also he likes the look of
Haunted Hall. Look at his answer to SAY
WHAT HE/SHE/IT NEEDS TEACHIN
MOST:

Our pup Throttler is a blot on
the family, he has gonn veggie. We
will pay big munny if you be strict
teachers and teach him back to
being a propper bludthirsty
weasly boy aggin.

Plus he has ticked the DEFFNLY box for doing the Entrance Test! Just wait till Uncle hears, he will go thrill thrill I bet.

Yours zestfully,
Littly

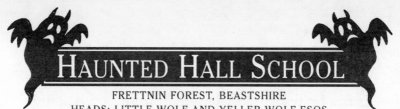

HAUNTED HALL SCHOOL

FRETTNIN FOREST, BEASTSHIRE
HEADS: LITTLE WOLF AND YELLER WOLF ESQS
DEPUTY HEAD: SMELLYBREFF WOLF ESQ
CARETAKER: STUBBS CROW ARKSQWIRE

Dear Mum and Dad,

I am all upset. I did not know wolfs are sposed to look down on weasels. But Uncle says they are common riffraff and much 2 easy to impress.

He says, **"YOU SEEM TO BE FORGETTING THAT I AM THE STAR ATTRACTION AND TERROR AROUND HERE! I DEMAND A BETTER CLASS OF CREATURE TO PRAISE MY SPLENDIDNESS."**

45

Oh boo, now Uncle says no more public appearances from him. Also no helping with Entrance Tests unless 1) we promise xtra helpings of bakebeans from now on, and 2) we gloom the place up a bit.

He says 2) is to remind him of his lovely grave, but really he is only letting off his spite. Just because we just finished getting HH all neat and cheery I bet!

Yours sinkingly,
Little

HAUNTED HALL SCHOOL

FRETTNIN FOREST, BEASTSHIRE
HEADS: LITTLE WOLF AND YELLER WOLF ESQS
DEPUTY HEAD: SMELLYBREFF WOLF ESQ
CARETAKER: STUBBS CROW ARKSQWIRE

Dear Mum and Dad,

Phew, just time for a short note because of working and working to make the place more gloomish. No more electric for us – Uncle says candles are heaps better for shivery shadows.

1 good thing has happened from this. Smells has stopped being Mister Woodcutter (lucky, because yesterday he unmade 6 beds in the dorm going chipchop with his chopper).

Now candles are his best thing and he wants us to call him Mister Waxworks. Because he chews candles up all soft and makes models. So far he has made just blobs but he calls them faymus stars off the telly, footballers, ect. Such a simple dimp.

Yours grownupply,

L Wolf

HAUNTED HALL SCHOOL

FRETTNIN FOREST, BEASTSHIRE
HEADS: LITTLE WOLF AND YELLER WOLF ESQS
DEPUTY HEAD: SMELLYBREFF WOLF ESQ
CARETAKER: STUBBS CROW ARKSQWIRE

Dear Mum and Dad,

So nice today! You would not *beleeev* how many answers to Kwestion Hares Stubbs has flown in. Lots of them say YES to paying large fees just for the chance to learn tuffness tricks and ghosty powers off us and Uncle!

Yeller is just back from a spider hunt. He has got buckets of fat tickly 1s, brilliant for making nice sticky webs plus hiding lurkingly down plugholes, inkwells, ect.

Stubbs helped me do a fine banner for waving from our flagpole on the belltower, saying:

HAUNTED HALL ENTRANCE TEST
This Sat at Ghosty time
Be there and have a good scare

Also we have done a fine job putting *eee-aaahs* in the doors. Next we must do some *creeeeks* in the floor, plus make all the radiators go *blugblug ticktap* in the night. Uncle will be all swole up with proudness I bet. So he will probly say:

GRRRR, I AM SO PLEASED I WILL SHOW YOU YOU MY POWER OF FINDING LOST TREASURE!

Smells is doing car alarm noises. He thinks it helps.

Yours deffly,
Little

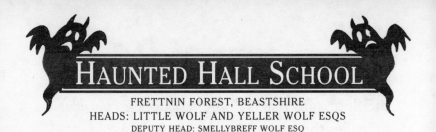

HAUNTED HALL SCHOOL

FRETTNIN FOREST, BEASTSHIRE
HEADS: LITTLE WOLF AND YELLER WOLF ESQS
DEPUTY HEAD: SMELLYBREFF WOLF ESQ
CARETAKER: STUBBS CROW ARKSQWIRE

Dear Mum and Dad,

Everything is ready for Entrance Test Day nearly, only 2 nights to go now.

Yeller has made the cellar a more dungeonish smell with old cabbage water plus poking cheesefur into cracks.

I went on a spooky chain hunt but not much luck. Just the 1s off our bikes, so not clanky enuff. BUT (big but) I have made all our family portraits of Uncles, Grandads ect a lot better. By putting swivelly eyes in them, they follow you round the room. Good, eh? My next job is make some secret panels so we can play Hide and Skweak. Get it?

Stubbs's clever beak has got Smells busy! Because, guess what? He made 2 Action–cub battlesuits, 1 is for him, 1 is for his ted. Also he put up the tent in the back garden. Arrroooo! Now Smells can live *outside* so not being in our way! He can chew his candles and make his waxworks plus do car alarm noises all he likes. Also going, "Bangbang, Mister Mozzy, Bangbang, Mister Ant, I got you, you are dead." ect.

Yours muchbetterly,
Little

HAUNTED HALL SCHOOL

FRETTNIN FOREST, BEASTSHIRE
HEADS: LITTLE WOLF AND YELLER WOLF ESQS
DEPUTY HEAD: SMELLYBREFF WOLF ESQ
CARETAKER: STUBBS CROW ARKSQWIRE

Dear Mum and Dad,

Tomorrow night is the night. *Crowds* of brutes are coming, so Uncle can have a good show off and we can have loads of fun. Stubbs is here saying, "Ark," meaning send a few arksamples, so I am.

Arksample 1, a small tortoise is coming. His mum thinks he is 2 shy so he needs a good shocking to get him a bit more out of his shell.

Arksample 2, Mister Webfoot is sending a jamjarfull of his frogspawn jellydots from the pond up by Lake Lemming. He thinks a scary school will help turn them into tadpoles.

52

Nextly, 3 fraidy bats. Their dad is fed up of buying nightlights and says can we get them used to the dark?

Plus Mrs Rattlesnake wants a lot of strictness for her young Squirmer. Because he has a bad habit of sucking his rattle and it gets 2 soggy.

Plus *loads* more have filled in our KHs. Also Smells has captured 6 bugs and insects that came creepingly to his tent. [He made a mini waxworks Chamber of Horrors on a tray to attract them. Then he went har har gotcha and popped them in his matchbox.]

Yours hummingly,
Mmm mm (guess who)

HAUNTED HALL SCHOOL

FRETTNIN FOREST, BEASTSHIRE
HEADS: LITTLE WOLF AND YELLER WOLF ESQS
DEPUTY HEAD: SMELLYBREFF WOLF ESQ
CARETAKER: STUBBS CROW ARKSQWIRE

Dear Mum and Dad,

Here is 1 of our Entrance Test papers for you to see:

ENTRANCE TEST PAPER
FOR HAUNTED HALL SCHOOL

TASK 1:
Sit quietly in the dark and wait for a ghost to pop out. No lickwashes, no scratching, no chewing test papers.

TASK 2:
When ghost comes, do your loudest WOO!

54

TASK 3:
See how quick you can dig a hole with an Entrance to it. Pop down it. Say, "Well done me, I have passed my Entrance, that was an easy test! Now I can be a pupil and give heaps of my dad's riches to Haunted Hall!"

TASK 4:
Pop back, then draw a nice pic of our Haunted Hall ghost.

TASK 5:
Learn the Haunted Hall School Song and sing fortissimo (your head off.) This is it:

   we are the Horrors of Haunted Hall
   Spooky are we, we are not scared at all
   No matter how tuff other brute beasts are
   we are more crafty so nah nah nah!

Do you like it? Now we are all ready and Uncle 2. We have said to him do not forget to appear just on the bong of midnight tomorrow night like normal. Only *do not be 2 scary* because remember 2 much jitters might make small brutes run away from Haunted Hall.

I am sure he will not appear 2 harshly. Because he promised, saying:

WHO ME? WOULD I?

Yours trustingly,

L

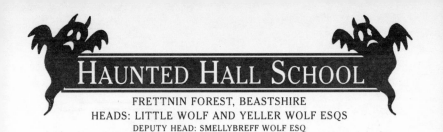

HAUNTED HALL SCHOOL

FRETTNIN FOREST, BEASTSHIRE
HEADS: LITTLE WOLF AND YELLER WOLF ESQS
DEPUTY HEAD: SMELLYBREFF WOLF ESQ
CARETAKER: STUBBS CROW ARKSQWIRE

Dear Mum and Dad,

I am all upset. Our Entrance Test was so good but then Smells and Uncle letted us down.

Such a big long line we had outside the front gate! And that was only just after the sun hid. By midnight, phew, what a wopping big crowd!

So Yeller and me did our Headly looks, saying (stern voices), "All hold hands in 2s, quickmarch and sit up straight in nice rows in the cellar." Also Stubbs did everso good caretaking. He did pulling the blinds down, mopping up sicks plus taking wrigglers to the toilets.

We let Smells stir the bakebeans in the pot, also give out some Test papers. Then guess what he went and did? He opened his matchbox up and said to his captured bugs and insects, "Hello,

I am Mister Sticker," then he glued them to the fridge.

That made all the other pupils go jumping about saying, "Help it's a trap! Help save me from being a fridge sticker!" ect.

Yeller said, "OO-ER, LET'S HOPE UNCLE REMEMBERS NOT TO BE 2 SCARY. SMELLS HAS MADE THESE PUPILS A BIT NERVOUS."

Up went the lovely steam of bakebeans, tempt tempt, from the pot. Then BONG came midnight. And all of a suddenly, right on time, Uncle appeared.

But he did not even *try* not to be 2 scary!
He did not come like a normal ghost
at all. He came in going

CRACKLE
FIZZ
FUME
FLASH!!

Because he was dressed
up as a big raging
forest fire!!!

From your feeless boy,
L Wolf

HAUNTED HALL SCHOOL

FRETTNIN FOREST, BEASTSHIRE
HEADS: LITTLE WOLF AND YELLER WOLF ESQS
DEPUTY HEAD: SMELLYBREFF WOLF ESQ
CARETAKER: STUBBS CROW ARKSQWIRE

Dear Mum and Dad,

Did I say about all our small pupils running away very very very very swiftly? Well, then Uncle said, **"GRRRAAA HAR HAR, WASN'T I FANTASTIC, THE WAY I MADE ALL THOSE SHINY PINK LITTLE BEASTS GO CHARGING BACK TO THEIR HOLES?"**

Yeller replied, "THEY WEREN'T PINK WHEN THEY CAME IN, THAT WAS ONLY BECAUSE YOU SHOCKED THEM OUT OF THEIR SKINS! LOOK AT ALL THESE LICKLE FURRY SUITS LYIN ABOUT ON THE FLOOR. NOW WE SHALL HAVE TO POST

THEM ALL BACK TO THEIR MUMS AND
DADS. AND NOT ALL OF THEM HAVE
GOT THEIR NAMES SEWN IN."

Uncle just larfed his hollow larf, saying,

**"HOOO HAR HAR, I HAVEN'T HAD
SUCH A GOOD TIME SINCE I DEVOURED
THE POSTMAN! BUT NOW TELL ME
HONESTLY, WASN'T I JUST TERRIFYING
AS A FOREST FIRE? DIDN'T YOU JUST
LOVE THE WAY I FRIGHTENED
THAT SKINNY GREY YOUNG
FELLOW? I MADE HIM
GO SCUTTLING
UP THE CHIMNEY!"**

I said, "Uncle, he was just a small shy tortoise.
You were sposed to bring him out of his shell
gently. But no, you made him go out pingingly
like a wet soap. It will take us ages fitting him

back in. And what about the Red Admiral butterfly you shocked into a Cabbage White?"

Uncle said, **"ANOTHER MASTERSTROKE! YES, I BELIEVE THAT HAPPENED WHEN I TRANSFORMED MYSELF INTO A PACK OF HOUNDS. CONGRATULATE ME SWIFTLY SWIFTLY ON THAT SPLENDIDLY DARK POWER! THAT WAS THE FIRST TIME I HAVE TRIED DIVIDING MYSELF AND BARKING IN MANY PLACES. MOST EFFECTIVE, WASN'T I? THANK YOU, THANK YOU!"**

I said, "But Uncle, you *promised* to appear gently. Those dark powers you did were 2 harsh."

Uncle said, **"STOP WHINING, VILE FLUFFBALL, YOU ARE GETTING ON MY**

NERVES, SPOILING MY HORRID FUN! AND
I WANT MORE! THOSE LITTLE SQUEAKERS
WERE FAR TOO EASY TO SCARE! THEY
ARE A WASTE OF GOOD TERROR, SO
NOW YOU MUST HAVE A BET WITH ME."

I said, "What sort of a bet, Uncle?"

He said, "I BET YOU MY POWER OF
FINDING LOST TREASURE THAT YOU
CAN'T FETCH ME ANY BRUTE BIG ENOUGH
OR BRAVE ENOUGH TO STAND UP TO ME
DOING MY DARKEST AND DIRTIEST,
SHALL WE SAY FOR 5 MINUTES?"

Yeller said, "BUT THAT IS A HARD BET
FOR US. WHAT IF WE LOSE?"

Uncle said, "TUFF! IF YOU LOSE, I SHALL
GO ALL SULKY AND NOT HELP YOU AT

ALL. AND THAT WILL SERVE YOU RIGHT FOR MAKING ME WORK SO HARD. I SHALL RETURN TO MY GRAVE FOREVER AND HAVE A WELL-DESERVED M.I.P.!"

I said, "But how can we have a Haunted Hall School without you?"

Uncle said, **"EXACTLY! NOW BE SILENT, SPECK! I WILL GIVE YOU 3 TURNS OF THE MOON TO SEARCH, NO MORE. GRRRAH HAR HAR!"**

Oh dear, Uncle is such a teaser.

Yours headscratchingly,

L

HAUNTED HALL SCHOOL

FRETTNIN FOREST, BEASTSHIRE
HEADS: LITTLE WOLF AND YELLER WOLF ESQS
DEPUTY HEAD: SMELLYBREFF WOLF ESQ
CARETAKER: STUBBS CROW ARKSQWIRE

The larder

Dear Mum and Dad,

Help! We have looked and looked in every hole and hollow tree in Frettnin Forest and not 1 brute is brave enuff to stand up to Uncle's powers. So now I must travel MILES afar to find such a rufftuff creature.

Yeller wants to come with me but I said no, Smells needs looking after. Also he must guard the school in case of robbers.

Uncle is horrid and lazy. Last night he could not be bothered going back to his grave even. He has moved into 1 of his old whisky bottles he found in the larder. Just because of it saying 'Powerful Spirit' on the label. He said:

So vain.

I must go to our library and look up
Tuff Creatures.

Yours studyingly,

L

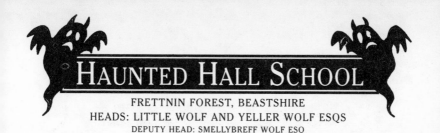

HAUNTED HALL SCHOOL

FRETTNIN FOREST, BEASTSHIRE
HEADS: LITTLE WOLF AND YELLER WOLF ESQS
DEPUTY HEAD: SMELLYBREFF WOLF ESQ
CARETAKER: STUBBS CROW ARKSQWIRE

The library

Dear Mum and Dad,

Cor, encyclopeeeeeeedias are fat, did you know that? They are so heavy you have to use both paws for holding and get Stubbs to sit on your head and turn the pages for you with his clever beak. Pity he is left-beaked because it made him start from Z and work backwards, so it took ages to get to A. And, oh no, A was just the letter we wanted for a rufftuff reptile!

Stubbs went, "Ark! Alark!!" meaning A is for Alarkgator!

Oo-er, so now I must find 1 and bring it back to win the bet against Uncle, save Haunted Hall School and discover the power to find my lost gold. But sad to say the nearest alarkgator lives many a mile away in Yellowsmoke Swamplands. That is in Grimshire! How can I get there, and back with an alarkgator, in just 3 turns of the moon? Yellowsmoke Swamplands takes 7 turns of the moon to run there and back, maybe 8!

Yours stumpedly,

L

HAUNTED HALL SCHOOL

FRETTNIN FOREST, BEASTSHIRE
HEADS: LITTLE WOLF AND YELLER WOLF ESQS
DEPUTY HEAD: SMELLYBREFF WOLF ESQ
CARETAKER: STUBBS CROW ARKSQWIRE

The dorm

Dear Mum and Dad,

Cannot sleep. Yeller has got paper all over the floor. He is scratching and scratching planningly with his pen. But 2 late I fear. Stubbs also is a busy widewaker. He is doing knitting plus making something from 1 of Yeller's inky plans. I do not know what, but there is canvas in it, also tentpoles, string, plus Yeller's kite with the wolf eyes on.

I think maybe they are both just taking their minds off us being poor and starving for ever. Because not even Yeller can think up a brilliant way to get to Yellowsmoke Swamplands AND come back with an alarkgator by Wensdie (cannot spell it).

Yours failedly,
Little

HAUNTED HALL SCHOOL

FRETTNIN FOREST, BEASTSHIRE
HEADS: LITTLE WOLF AND YELLER WOLF ESQS
DEPUTY HEAD: SMELLYBREFF WOLF ESQ
CARETAKER: STUBBS CROW ARKSQWIRE

Under tree in front garden

Dear Mum and Dad,

Something gulpish. Are you ready? Gulp.
Stubbs says he wants to *fly* me to seek for an
alarkgator!

He says, "Ark!" meaning Arkshun Stations!
Also he says two new tail feathers have come, so
his flying is strong.

I said, "But Stubbs, you are only a crowchick,
not a full fledgie even, are you sure you can carry
a passenger? Besides, how will we get a big ruff
tuff reptile back here in just 3 turns of the moon?"

He just says, "Ark!" meaning do not worry, he is an arkspert at flying now. Also he has made a thing from Yeller's plan that is a secret invention to help us. But no time to arksplain now.

Yeller is a bit upset not to come, but he must stay and do guarding in case of robbers, plus being minder of Smells.

Our crunchy snacks are packed and I just put on my string harness that Stubbs knitted. We are ready. I just want to say a small message for my grave in case of emerjuncy:

Here lies L. Wolf
He fell off the sky
He was a bit 2 heavy
but never mind,
good try.

Your trembly boy,
Little

Dear Mum and Dad,

Sorry about the scribbul, this is a flying airletter. We are up. Aayee, I love highuppness it is so thrilly, kiss kiss! The wind takes your breff and pins your ears and fur back. Stubbs is a strong airswimmer but getting bit tired now. Frettnin Forest is like moss below.

Now we are over the Parching Plain. It is bumpy. Stubbs says, "Ark!" meaning arkstra hot air because of the burning sands. So bouncy.

Poor Stubbs, I think he has got the

Wing

a c h e

Dear Mum and Dad,

We did a crashland, a dusty 1, but our bones stayed together. Lucky us, eh? So hot here, phew! I am trying to make a shadow so Stubbs can sleep cool and get his strongness up. I wanted to read about Yeller's invention. There is a paper with it called 'Instruckshuns', but my head is busy having thinks. Are there some tuff and fearless brutes that live in parching plains? Maybe, and then no need to fly further, eh?

My thinks are up in the sky above now. I can hear buzzards saying *keeee-keeee* in case we are a nice snack for them. Oo-er, I remember now, buzzards are v fierce with hooks for claws, also sharp beaks. Ding! An idea has just jumped in my head! I will play dead and try to capture 1 when it comes down to eat me.

Yours backsoonly (I hope),
Little Snack (just kidding)

Dear Mum and Dad,

Cor, I did not like that buzzard coming up close. I made my eyes slits but I saw him looking at my tasty parts. So I said, "'Scuse me, I am just a small beakful and my friend here is also. P'raps you would like to come back with us and meet my Uncle. He is a lot bigger."

The buzzard said, "Kee-keee! How big is hee-ee?"

I said, "Very big, p'raps you have heard of him, his name is BB Wolf."

And do you know what?
Off he went, *VOOOM*. Such a
big softy. Lucky the wind of him
voooming made Stubbs nice and cool.
He is feeling a lot better!

Yours Readyfortakeoffly,
Little

74

The sky, cloudy bit over some mountains

Dear Mum and Dad,

Brr, Broken Tooth Caves and Grim Mountains far under us. Can see roofs small as sparrownests, Hamneezia maybe. So frozz up here now. Stubbs is flapping very hard. I must stop writing and make myself streamliney.

Yours cheeks suckedinly,

75

Dear Mum and Dad,

Oo-er, I fell asleep for a bit. When I woke up I thought, "Oh no, I have turned into a polar bear cub sitting on a big seagull!" But do not fret and frown, it was just us flying through a blizzard.

1 good thing, it will be a soft crash if we do fall because the White Wildness is all snow. But paws crossed Stubbs can keep going as the crow flies, eh?

Yours fridgly,
Brittle (joke)

Dear Mum and Dad,

Phew, landed
hardly at
Yellowsmoke
Swamplands,
but not
crashingly
because of
swamp. But
now a bit mucky.
Stubbs is my hero.

We are trying out Yeller's new invention – a
Tentyglider, it's brilliant! The Instruckshuns are
quite hard, but if you fold it 1 way you can do
camping in it (the door is Yeller's kite with the
yellow wolf eyes on). And if you fold it a new
way, it turns into a glider. So Stubbs can tow
even wopping grate brutes in it!

Camping out is my worst thing, even with
Stubbs for company. Bad things happen in the

night. Like you hear the bogeywolf coming up the stairs to get you. He goes *step step step step step*. Then you wake up and you think, phew, no stairs in here, it was just a squirrel plopping nuts onto the roof.

More later from,

Yours widerwakely,

Little

Dear Mum and Dad,

Later. No alarkgators yet, but we did find a lion. He was hiding in the long grass. Stubbs was upset because he had feathers on his tongue, so we did not go 2 near.

I shouted out to him a 'scuse me, saying, "Hmm, I do not 'spect you ever get scared, do you?"

He said, "SSPITTT RRRUMBLE GGRRRAAA! RRRRidiculous idea!"

But when I said about coming with us to our cellar to stand up to Uncle Bigbad's shocking powers for 5 minutes he said, "Er, d'you mean Bigbad Wolf? Oh, dribbly feller, very bad temper? Um, well you see, I must have my wide open spaces. Otherwise I would come with you and do my bit for the Pride, I honestly would. But cellars, no no, much too closed in, you follow me? And no lovely long grasses to tickle my tummy. Goodbye." Then he ran away.

Getting darkly dim now, but still, Mum always says: *Yellow eyes are friends with the dark.* So handy about our yellow wolf-eye door which is nice and scary. Also lucky our camp is on an island (they are safe from sharp teeth). Wish we had some islands in Frettnin Forest.

Yours yawnly plus an "Ark" from Stubbs,

Little

Yellowsmoke Swamplands, on an island in a lake

Dear Mum and Dad,

You want to be careful about islands. Because sometimes they are alarkgators. And when you get up in the morning, better not go, "Hmm, breakfast, yum." Just in case your island starts thinking breakfast thoughts 2.

Also, if you see a sort of green bridge going up in front of your eyes, do not walk across, it might be the alarkgator opening his mouth. Better if you stay where you are on his back and say, "Good thing I put this tent up on you because cor, it makes you look so hansum." (Rule 3 of Badness, fib your head off.)

I did hear a funny *vrroomba vrroomba* in my ear in the night, but 2 tired and cosy to get wurrid. Then this morning I found out the alarkgator just ate a small cub that was listening to his Walkwolf. That is Y his words have got a beat, like, "Jump in my pool, it's really cool."

I said, "Hello, I am L Wolf Esqwire and this is S Crow Arksqwire. We are here to tell you about a nice prize you have won in a raffle. It is a trip on a glider to visit a funny school. Would you like to come?" (More Rule 3.)

The alarkgator said:
"You don't fool me with your talk about a raffle ha!
Get in my jaws and let me snaffle ya!"

I said, "You are very rufftuff. Are you scared of anybody? Like a wolf maybe?"

The alarkgator said:
"My name is Snap, I am where it's at
I'm a cool cool alligator.
I am the jaw you can't ignore
Catch you now, or catch you later!

Hope you don't mind if I say to you
You'd be mighty good to chew.
You look tasty, you look crunchy
How would you like to be my lunchy?"

I said, "Oh, all right." Because I remembered
another 1 of Mum's best sayings, the 1 about
how to get untangled if you are in a prickly
bush. She always says: *You must give to the
blackberry bush before he'll let you go.* So I held
Stubbs by the wing and we jumped in
the alarkgator's mouth. And
guess what I gave him?
Answer, the
tentpole!

Arrroooo! He lashed and splashed and
splashed and lashed but he *could* not eat me and
Stubbs for his lunchy, har har.

Yours unchewedly,
Little

Dear Mum and Dad,

Do you know what? That alarkgator was just a big baby! He cried and cried just because me and Stubbs tricked him with the tentpole and he could not eat us. So no good us gliding *him* back to HH to stand up to Uncle, because he would probly say "Boohoo blub" straight away, then Uncle would win his bet, boo shame.

Now me and Stubbs are all glim and glumly. Because 2 turns of the moon have gone already! We had a chat and we said shame, Grimshire is a bit rubbish, better go back to Beastshire. So Stubbs said, "Ark!" meaning arkay with him.

He had to fly us back across The White Wildness, then over Mount Tester to Broken Tooth Caves. So hard for him, but on and on he flew flappingly with no moaning. Also we hit the land gentle as a leaf.

Sometimes you get outlaws here but I 'spect we will not see any. We have made the Tentyglider into a glider just in case. Now off we go into the caves with our torches going flash.

Yours searchingly,

L

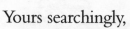

Dear Mum and Dad,

No luck finding outlaws but guess what?
A Mountain Ranger has come to help us. He
has got sharp eyes, a pointy face and a smell like
pepper. His uniform is nice but sticky out at
the back.

He spoke softly to us
saying, "You look like
smart young chappies
and I have some
questions for you. Will
you gaze into my eyes
and answer them?"

We did not know how to say no to him. So
we said all about searching for a large brute that
is not afraid of a certain faymus terror. He said,
"My boys, you interest me strangely. Am I to
understand that you are referring to that terrible
crook and miser, Bigbad Wolf? Him, as they say,
'wot died of the jumping beanbangs'."

I said a proud, "Yes," and Stubbs said, "Ark," meaning I arkgree with Little.

The Ranger said, "Amazing! What is his racket now?"

I said, "He does not play tennis, he is a shocking ghost and master of spirit dizgizzes. Also Star Attraction at Haunted Hall, the scaryest school in the world."

The Ranger said, "And where exactly is his residence?"

I said, "He has a v nice grave, but just lately he has moved into a whisky bottle in the larder at Haunted Hall. But when us 2 can find a beast that is not scared of him for 5 minutes, he will say by Spirit Power where all my gold is hiding. So I will be rich wunce morely."

Then the Ranger got very peppery, and he said that was *very* interesting. Now, arrroooo, he says he knows a way to help us! Because he knows a brute beast that is not scared of *anything*. All we have got to do is go with him to the edge of a very steep cliff and wink down his telescope.

Good, I hate steepness, but I like telescopes. More later.

Your nosy boy,
Little

Dear Mum and Dad,

Sorry about the nervous writing, there is a bear, it is big

(behind us).

Yrs goodbyfreverly,
L Wolf

Bears' camp near a fast river, Dark Hills, Beastshire

Dear Mum and Dad,

Oh no, we are captured by bears, and it's all that Ranger's fault!

We were on a path just a small way down from the top of a

s

t

e

e

p cliff.

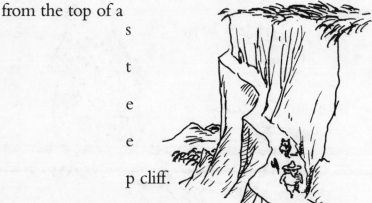

The Ranger said for us to look peepingly through the telescope at a boy and girl cub. They were standing in a roary river, fishing for salmon. You would not *beleeeev* how strong they are for cubs! Also they gave each other such fierce bites and cuffs! The mum bear was there but she was 2 busy scoffing honeycakes to watch them.

That Ranger was silly. He would not be still!
He kept standing up so the sun went flash on his
shiny buttons. Also he kept doing loud coffs.

I said, "You want to be careful, this path is
thin. Just spose a huge big brute comes up
behind, there is only room for 1 of us to escape
quick!"

That was when Stubbs went, "Ark!
Ick!" meaning arkscape quick!
Because the dad bear
(wopping huge) was right
behind us holding my
tail in a tight squeeze.
And guess who
escaped quick?
(Clue, not me
or Stubbs.)
Answer, the
Ranger!

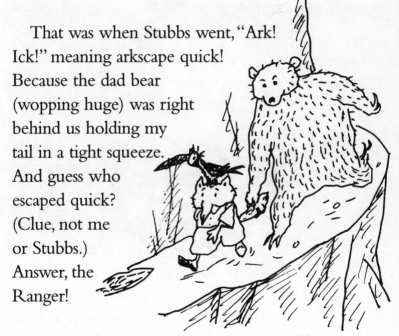

But just then came a loud scream. Stubbs
shouted, "Ark!" meaning arkcident. The boy cub
got swept away by the roary river. Quick as a

chick I said to the bear, "Let go my tail and we
will save your cub." So he did.

Now I know, Dad, you will say, "Whyo Y are
you still captured? Y not flee away quick and say
'Har har I was fibbing my head off'?" Answer,
we need that cub!

Yours daringdeedly,
Little

Dear Mum and Dad,

The boy cub nearly got drownded in the
rapids. But Stubbs dropped me on him in the
water with Yeller's strong kite string tied to my
harness. I bited hold of the fur on the bear cub's
neck. Then Stubbs gave the other end of the
string to the dad bear. Even the lazy mum bear
stopped scoffing and came to pull.

The dad and mum bear pulled and pulled,
then PLOP, out of the roary water we came.

The dad bear whacked the boy bear 2 good
1s, saying, "THAT's for being stupid and THAT's
for next time." Then the mum bear whacked
him a hard 1 also. Then the girl cub bit him,
then he bit her back. And do you know what he
said? He said, "Rocks and rapids can't scare me!
I like banging my head on rocks! I did that on
purpose, so there!" And he gave me a hard push
out of the way and climbed up a tall tall tree.

His mum said, "Get down out of that tree, Normus! There are bees in that nest, they'll sting you all over!"

The boy cub said, "Bees don't scare me, I like getting stinged." Then he got stings in his nose plus on his black tongue even and he just said, "Har har, doesn't hurt!"

It did really, he was just showing off. Also he threw the hive at me for a joke to make the bees chase me.

That is Y I said we need that bear. He is a big bully, but I think he can win the bet against Uncle! I just hope his mum and dad will let him go with me and Stubbs.

Yours hopingly,
Little

Dear Mum and Dad,

I think the Bears have got more nasty tempers than Dad. (Not really, only kidding Dad, yours is the baddest.) So it was quite easy to take Normus away from them. Because he gets on their nerves a lot. Also they say they do not know what to do with him. Maybe that is Y they did not eat me, plus they liked listening about me being a wolf cub, also a proud Co-Head of Haunted Hall School.

Mr Bear said to me, "So you're a wolf cub and he's a crowchick, eh? Funny that, because I thought maybe you was just somethink wot the cat coffed up! And you're starting up a school, you say? Now I don't see that. I don't see you being a teacher at all. Wot I see is you covered in honey and spread on my sandwich. Unless you can prove you ain't telling me big fat fibs!"

Quick as a chick I said, "Pay attention, claws on lips, come along come along!" like we did for practiss on the chestnuts.

Mrs Bear said, "Oo, he knows all the sayings, just like a proper teacher! Do some more!"

I said, "Now then, sit up straight, no chewing."

She said, "Oo, ain't he luvly? Go on, Dad bear, let's send Normus away to his school. After all, he never learns nuffink off of us, does he?"

Dad bear said, "How do we know it's a proper strict school with the right sort of School Spirit and all that?"

I said, "Haunted Hall has got the strictest most shockingest School Spirit in Beastshire. His name is BB Wolf."

Dad bear said, "Well that's all right then. And do you believe in short sharp shocks?"

I said, "Oh yes."

Dad bear said, "Good. Just what he needs. The only way to get sense into him is to knock it in. So don't take no cheek off of him. Show him the back of your paw. And a good sharp bite never does him no harm. Does it, Normus?"

But Normus wasn't listening. He was wrestling with his sister for a tin of peaches (canteen size). He grabbed it off her and opened it. Sideways. With his claws. Oo-er.

Stubbs has finished putting the glider together. Hope Normus does not break it with his strongness.

Yours pawscrossedly,

Dear Mum and Dad,

Such hard flying for Stubbs! He had me in the harness plus towing the glider behind. Phew, what a shouter that Normus is. Nearly loud as Yeller. He kept shouting, "Higher higher! Gliding can't scare me!"

It was dark 2, also some cold rain spit.

Over Windy Ridge flapped Stubbs. The air was so bumpy and frozz, it was like a fight all the way to Lake Lemming. We were a bit wurrid when we got there, about no runway. Also all the dark trees on the edge of Frettnin Forest.

But good old Yeller. He was thinking of us in the night. He did not want us going bash into a tree. So he said to Smells, "QUICK MISTER

WAXWORKS!
RUN TO THE
SHORE OF THE
LAKE WITH YOUR
CANDLES AND YOUR
SHOVEL! WE MUST MAKE
2 TONS OF MOLEHILLS
AND PUT LIGHTS ON THEM."

That made a nice landing place and
down went Stubbs and the glider behind
with Normus on it, all smooth and crashless.

Stubbs and me did 3 arrroooos for joy and
said, "Well done and thanks, Yeller and Smells!"
But not Normus. He just gave Yeller a
Chinese burn, saying, "Flying can't scare
me! I like crashing!" Then
he said to Smells, "Hello,
Stickybud, let's
play Head in
Mouth, bags
you go 1st!"

Smells did not stay. He gave Normus 1 of his nasty looks. Then he took the shovel and ran off quick as a chick to his tent in the back garden.

I said to Normus, "No time for rufftuff games, we must hurry to school before midnight OR ELSE."

He just said, "OR ELSE *what*? Can't make me. Teachers can't scare me."

I said, "Good thing 2. Plus I hope you are not scared of Uncle Bigbad either!"

Yours wishmeluckly,
Little

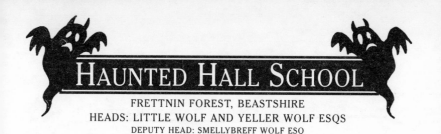

HAUNTED HALL SCHOOL

FRETTNIN FOREST, BEASTSHIRE
HEADS: LITTLE WOLF AND YELLER WOLF ESQS
DEPUTY HEAD: SMELLYBREFF WOLF ESQ
CARETAKER: STUBBS CROW ARKSQWIRE

Dear Mum and Dad,

Back we went rushingly to Haunted Hall. We needed to hot up bakebeans in a pot quick.

Haunted Hall was all glum and glim and gloomy, but Normus did not seem to be 1 bit nervous. He just kept barging us saying, "Let's have a wrestle," ect, also getting in our way a lot.

Then Stubbs said, "Ark!" meaning hark, the bong of midnight! But Normus did not be still. He pulled a big bunch of nice new feathers out of Stubbs's tail. Such a big bully!

Then all of a suddenly, Uncle came swooshingly out of his whisky bottle, more glowy and horrible than before even.

He did Hollow Larfs plus Terrible Screams, then some new Terrible Words:

**SNIFF SNUFF SNARE, I SMELL BEAR!!
SNIFF SNUFF SNUP, I WILL EAT HIM UP!!**

Normus went a bit quiet. But then he said, "Ghosts can't scare me! I'm a *big* bear, I like shocks!"

So Uncle went, **"RRRRRAAAAARRRR!"** And he did his Forest Fire and his Pack of Hounds and his Swarm of Killer Bees.

But Normus just said, "Can't scare me, I can be nasty like that, look!" And he gave 3 hard kicks, 1 for me, 1 for Yeller, 1 for Stubbs. Then he sat on us. V hardly.

Uncle said, **"HOO HAR HAR, I KNEW IT! HE'S BLINKING BLUNKING TERRIFIED OF ME."**

But he wasn't really.

Yours squashedly,
Little

HAUNTED HALL SCHOOL

FRETTNIN FOREST, BEASTSHIRE
HEADS: LITTLE WOLF AND YELLER WOLF ESQS
DEPUTY HEAD: SMELLYBREFF WOLF ESQ
CARETAKER: STUBBS CROW ARKSQWIRE

Dear Mum and Dad,

What a big cheater Uncle is! I wrote a message on the back of a stamp and posted it in his whisky bottle for him to read. It said:

Then out came his ghosty voice saying,

"GRRRRAAAAH, LAST NIGHT DOES NOT COUNT, I WAS NOT EVEN TRYING TO BE A TERROR, BUT JUST YOU WAIT! TONIGHT I SHALL SCARE THE BEAR'S FUR OFF!!"

Oh boo, I forgot Rule of Badness number 9: NEVER trust a big bad wolf.

Yours cheatedly,
Silly me

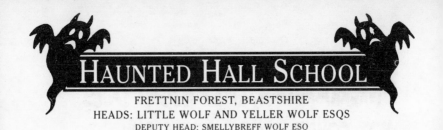

HAUNTED HALL SCHOOL

FRETTNIN FOREST, BEASTSHIRE
HEADS: LITTLE WOLF AND YELLER WOLF ESQS
DEPUTY HEAD: SMELLYBREFF WOLF ESQ
CARETAKER: STUBBS CROW ARKSQWIRE

Dear Mum and Dad,

Oo-er, Uncle was so scary in the night! He did The Crawling Paw. He made the paw go creepingly up the wall by itself outside the dorm window. Then it went *scritch scratch* with its nails. It made me call out, "Oo-er, help! Where are you, Stubbs and Yeller?" But no need to ask because I found out all of a suddenly they were tucked up tight right next to me!

Then I said, "Where is Normus?" Answer, fast asleep. Not 1 bit nervous even. Ah, but then he had to get up to go to the loo. The dark was deep and the floorboards did *ee-arrs*. We held our breaths waiting for a big shock. Then Normus pulled the chain and we heard:

"SSSSHHHHHHHAAAAAAH"!

Har har, that was Uncle
jumping out of the
toilet being a Terror!

But Normus just
went back to bed
yawningly. He did not
bother to light a candle even. Also before he got
back in bed he went donk on our heads with
the toilet brush saying, "That's for you becuz I
hate your toilet. But toilets can't scare me, so
there!"

Yours lumply,
Little

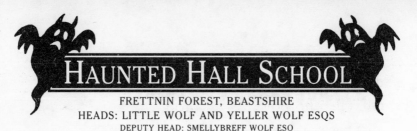

Haunted Hall School

FRETTNIN FOREST, BEASTSHIRE
HEADS: LITTLE WOLF AND YELLER WOLF ESQS
DEPUTY HEAD: SMELLYBREFF WOLF ESQ
CARETAKER: STUBBS CROW ARKSQWIRE

Dear Mum and Dad,

Hope you can read this, I am see-through
(Yeller and Stubbs 2!) So maybe my ink is also!
Shall I say how? Answer, training by Uncle in
secret powers!

He has really got his temper up now. I was
having a small zizz on the table-tennis table. It was
still daytime, not near Uncle's haunting hours.
But he broke the ghost rule and came out of his
bottle to give me a message. He was 2 cross 2
stand still so he dressed up as a pingpong ball and
used me as a net. He said:

Now I will tell you about Uncle's training. It's easy cheesy! All you do is hold on to a ghost's tail. Then his powers run through you (all tickly) and you can stay see-through till the 1st cockodoodle of the dawning.

You can go 1-2-3 Pop! And off comes your head. Or you can do a little hop and up you go floatingly like a small cloud. Hmm, nice feeling.

So in the deep dark, Uncle whispered, "FOLLOW ME." Up we went floatingly through the ceiling of the dorm going "WOO!" We went through all the beds, furniture ect, plus we made all Normus' bedclothes go walking round him. And our best thing was turning into small skeletons. Because then we got in the biscuit tin by Normus' bed and did a very noisy tapdance, har har!

Normus jumped out of bed. Not because of terror, oh no. He said, "Spooks and skellingtons can't scare me. I am tuff, I am ruff. Now I am going outside to bash up Smellybreff!"

What can we do to stop him?

Yours triedeverythingly,
   L Wolf

PS. uncle is no help, he just says TUFF. Sorry.

HAUNTED HALL SCHOOL

FRETTNIN FOREST, BEASTSHIRE
HEADS: LITTLE WOLF AND YELLER WOLF ESQS
DEPUTY HEAD: SMELLYBREFF WOLF ESQ
CARETAKER: STUBBS CROW ARKSQWIRE

Dear Mum and Dad,

Did you think to yourself hmm, I was wondering Y Smells took that shovel when he ran off? Me 2. Answer, he went to his tent with it for digging a bear trap! So he did not get bashed after all, arrroooo.

We all peeped over the edge. Normus was down nice and deep. He saw us peeping and said, "Traps can't scare me. I will get out any minute, then I will bite you hard."

Yeller said, "TRUE. PLUS HE WILL SQUASH US AGAIN I BET. QUICK LET'S GET ALL STRICT!"

Stubbs said, "Ark! Wark!" meaning yes he is so arkward he deserves a hard whack. Also Smells wanted to be Mister Hunter and donk him with his chopper.

But I said, "No, no more bashing."

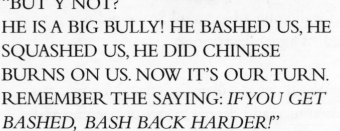

Yeller said, "BUT Y NOT? HE IS A BIG BULLY! HE BASHED US, HE SQUASHED US, HE DID CHINESE BURNS ON US. NOW IT'S OUR TURN. REMEMBER THE SAYING: *IF YOU GET BASHED, BASH BACK HARDER!*"

I said, "But everybody bashes Normus. It doesn't do any good. His mum bashes him, his dad bashes him, even his sister bashes him."

Stubbs said, "Ark! Shark!" meaning he needs a short sharp shock, he pulled out my best feathers!

I said, "No more bashing, no more shocks, no

more strictness. This is what we'll do." I did an important whisper to all the chums and off they went thinkingly to work.

Then I said down the bear trap, "Normus, are you listening? We are going to fetch a ladder to let you up."

Normus just said, "Good, becuz then I can squash your heads in."

Yours oo-erly,
Little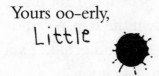

HAUNTED HALL SCHOOL

FRETTNIN FOREST, BEASTSHIRE
HEADS: LITTLE WOLF AND YELLER WOLF ESQS
DEPUTY HEAD: SMELLYBREFF WOLF ESQ
CARETAKER: STUBBS CROW ARKSQWIRE

Dear Mum and Dad,

Da-daaah! Just in case you thought oh no our boy is killed dead by a head squash, here I am again.

Because listen what happened. We got ready, then we put the ladder down the trap. Normus started climbing up going grrr and grufff. I said, "Normus, have you ever had a chum?"

He said, "Wot's a chum?"

I said, "You know, a friend, or somebody that likes you and only does pretend bites."

Normus said, "No, I haven't got 1, everybody hates me."

114

I said, "Aha, that was *before*. This is *after*. So come out now and have your surprise."

Normus said, "I know surprises, they are donks on my head!"

I said, "No, no donking. Listen, I like you, Yeller likes you, Stubbs likes you. You have won a bet and now we will be rich because you are the only brute beast in Beastshire with the braveness to stand up to Uncle Bigbad."

Yeller held out a stiff paper with all writing on in nice colours done by him, saying, "NORMUS BEAR, I PRESENT YOU WITH A STIFFKIT OF BRAVENESS. WELL DONE. AND BECAUSE YOUR READING IS A BIT RUBBISH, I WILL SAY THE WORDS FOR YOU."

Then he read:

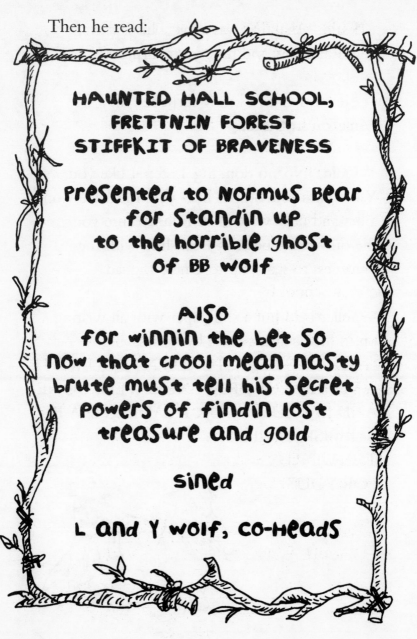

HAUNTED HALL SCHOOL,
FRETTNIN FOREST
STIFFKIT OF BRAVENESS

Presented to Normus Bear
for standin up
to the horrible ghost
of BB Wolf

Also
for winnin the bet so
now that crool mean nasty
brute must tell his secret
powers of findin lost
treasure and gold

sined

L and Y Wolf, co-Heads

Normus said, "You mean, you really like *me*. Even the crow? Even that small diggy cub with the shovel?"

I said, "Well, not Smells, no. He hates everybody. But the rest of us."

A big tear fell off Normus' nose and he said, "This is the best, most scaryest school I know. I'm not going home. Ever. I want to stay and have chums."

And we said all right then, you can be our 1st proper pupil. Then Stubbs flew up to the belltower and gave the bell a hard ding for Haunted Hall's 1st proper daytime lesson: Spooksuit Making.

Yours proudly,
L Wolf Esqwire
(Co-Head)

HAUNTED HALL SCHOOL

FRETTNIN FOREST, BEASTSHIRE
HEADS: LITTLE WOLF AND YELLER WOLF ESQ
DEPUTY HEAD: SMELLYBREFF WOLF ESQ
CARETAKER: STUBBS CROW ARKSQWIRE

Normal Boring School

Dear Mum and Dad,

Big shock! We took Normus into the larder to meet Uncle in his whisky bottle, also to say come on, be a sport, pay up your bet. But oh no, a burglar has been and done stealing! It was while we were all in the back garden. And guess what he ~~burglard stealed burguled~~ pinched? Answer, the whisky bottle!

Oh boo, now we will never find out the power of finding lost treasure. Also, that is the end of Haunted Hall. Because the burglar has got the 'haunted' part, in other words, Uncle! Boo shame, because Normus will probly think we are now just a normal boring school and go home.

Yours startagainly,

L

118

Dear Mum and Dad,

Thank you for your LOUD LETTER saying about the shame of losing our best relative. You say will he ever Moan in Peace again? Also you say I have let down the name of the pack, so Dad has gone all sulkish. He says he will not come and visit us here *ever*, not till his lost bruv is back in his happy haunting ground.

OK, I will try my hardest to do hunting for that burglar. Off I trot.

Yours scentingly,
    Little the tracker

Dear Mum and Dad,

All I have found so far is 1 will-of-the-whisker down the marshy end of the forest. Also 2 bad pongs, but sad to say made by skunks, not Uncle. Yeller came and found me. He has not found Uncle either. He says Smells is all upset. He took the stuffing out of his ted to look, in case Uncle was hiding in there, but no luck. Now, just because he put the stuffing back wrong, he says Yeller stealed ted and left behind a fat tortoise.

Stubbs says he will help restuff ted proply, but not just yet. Because when he was highflying about looking down owlholes he bonked into a branch. So a sore beak for Stubbs too, boo shame. Plus Normus got his head wedged in a tin of peaches. Maybe he thought Uncle wanted a bath in peach juice.

Will we ever find Uncle's trail?

Yours lipnibblingly,
Little

Dear Mum and Dad,

As I said, no luck yesterday, but today everybody went round the house clueing with magnifying glasses plus notebooks and sharp pencils. We got v tired and v feddup. But by teatime, bit by bit, everybody found maybe 1 small cluelet:

Smells found 1 foxy pawprint (found in rosebed outside larder window).

Normus found 2 red whiskers.

Stubbs found 1 toggle off of a Ranger's jacket.

Yeller found 1 nose smudge on a custardskin in the larder.

And I found 1 Ranger's hat that made me sneezy.

Add them all up and they = 1 greedy Ranger with red whiskers and a smell like pepper that knows about Uncle Bigbad's power of finding lost treasure.

I said, "Hmm, let me think. That is just like the Mountain Ranger who let me get captured by Normus' dad! He was peppery. Also I noticed his coat was bulgy at the back. Oo-er! Now I know who that was! He was not a Ranger at all. He was that Wanted crook and Master of Dizgizzes (cannot spell it), MISTER TWISTER!"

Yours,
Sherlock Wolf (get it?)

The Yelloweyes Forest Detective Agency

Dear Mum and Dad,

Normus says clue hunts are his best game ever
and never mind about Haunted Hall closing but
can he be in our pack? He likes being our chum
but also he wants to be a detective. Good, eh?

So from now on we
are all going to do
solving crimes and
mysteries all over the
forest. So no more
schools, no more
horrors, no more
Haunted Hall.

We are The Yelloweyes Forest Detectives!

THE YELLOWEYES FOREST DETECTIVE AGENCY

Detectives: LW Wolf and Yeller Wolf
Flying Squad: Stubbs Crow
Large Clue Hunter: Normus Bear
Small Clue Hunter: Smellybreff Wolf

Tracking Tricking Dizgizzing
our speciality

So look out you big robbers and crooks like Mister Twister. The YFDA is on your trail!

Yours elementary-my-dear-mum-and-dadly,
L Wolf, Forest Detective

Le end

[french]